LETTERS TO MY FATHER

poems by

Juanita Kirton

Finishing Line Press
Georgetown, Kentucky

LETTERS TO MY FATHER

ACKNOWLEDGMENTS

Previous Published from this collection

Blue (love letter to my son)~~*Stone Canoe*. Spring, 2017.
Fall Shoe Skates~~ *Persimmon* Tree, Short Takes. Summer, 2015.
Father's Day~~*Mom Egg Magazine*. Summer, 2015.
Rage~~*Mom Egg Magazine*. Spring, 2019.
Snap-Shot~~*Alexandria Publication*, Online Portfolio. April 2018.
The Backs on Which I Stand~~*Rats Ass Review*. Spring, 2017.
Wednesday's (Every Wednesday re-titled)~~*Mom Egg Magazine*. Winter,
2016.

Publisher: Leah Maines
Editor: Christen Kincaid
Cover Art and Design: Terreyl TL Kirton
Author Photo: Terreyl TL Kirton

Order online: www.finishinglinepress.com
also available on amazon.com

Author inquiries and mail orders:
Finishing Line Press
P. O. Box 1626
Georgetown, Kentucky 40324
U. S. A.

Table of Contents

Listen

Father taught me to listen inside a conch shell
Seize scent from the ocean
Wait for the wave
Swim with flying fish
        Change a tire, the oil

Mother taught me to stir love into flour
Braid hair   piano lessons
Recite a poem
Drive far to forget
Hold a family secret

Daddy wore stiff white shirts
Drove Cadillac's
Played Cricket
I danced on his shoes
He touched me in the dark

Mummy loved to dance
Dominate Bid Whist   fried codfish cakes
Strip wallpaper
Church attendance a must   wore gloves
Ignored betrayal   forgot to listen

Daddy was visible
Mummy lingered in blindness
Daddy said, "Don't tell"
Mummy remained silent
I didn't tell
Mummy and daddy   speechless

Dear Daddy

Sorry

        I was

                not perfect

Regret

        you couldn't   stay

           just

         my daddy

HANDS

One hand, cradled his newborn little girl and he loved her.

    His hands, held her hands and she perfected her first steps and he loved her.

        His hand, took her hand and entrusted her to school. He would miss her.

    His hands invited her to dream, unbounded potential. He was proud of her.

    His hands guided her feet and she ran marathons of hope, living fearlessly.

    His hands withdrew her panties and touched her exposed innocent skin.

        His hands led her hand to the secret   her heart broke.

        She is untouchable.

The Shower

White and sticky
smeared across my belly
faint scent
soiling innocence

Wash and bathe
no emancipation

Dirty little girl
daddy's little girl

mummy's girl child
vanished girlhood

Every Wednesday

Fry up some codfish cakes
with Bajan hot sauce
water set to boil
      cup of yellow corn meal
      chop okra
      salt with a pinch
      blend and swirl
      mix and fold
      lower the heat

Brooklyn Brownstones, 1950's
Grandma stirs *cou-cou*
the air is heavy
perspiration drips into the pot
rendering more brine
she stirs in love
tweaks and nurtures

We eat steamy *cou-cou* on Wednesdays
daddy's mommy sings my name
It drapes above the vapors
I sit on 2-phone books to reach
brother tugs at mommy's right nipple
eight years   two more will extract the last drops
eight years   grandma's son steals my song
the steam dissolves
I am invisible
grandma no longer stirs *cou-cou*.

BAKES

Kitchen aromas crowd three corners
one reeks of shadows
no one sees   no one hears
upside down   painted clown

Mother gripped the old black cast iron handle
with ease the batter spoons
hitting the oil
entrance of flour stretches
Bakes for snack   puffy and hot
savory with sugar and spice
mommy fries them nice

Bakes keep coming
mother continues her ritual
blinded by fear
four mouths to sustain

her hunger deferred

Untitled

I bled into the back seat

        Shadows followed me

My womb carried a lullaby

        I wrote letters to you

Listened to Billy and Ella

        I sang like Sarah Vaughan

Lost my sight
Lost my taste
Lost mummies lullaby

FATHER'S DAY

Lessons on forgiveness leaked into her navel
harsh messages pierced her body
the welcome laughter of a tickle   twisted   uninvited
stolen

In silence she screamed   wrong
mother refused to see   refused to hear
forgive the gift of blindness
childhood days lost in shadows
like *Maya A.*   her voice stilled
who would care   who wants a dirty little girl?

The father made-up the dead
with stiff white shirts and dark suits
he counseled young men
church leader   community chief
master of the house
his hands left dents inside her casing
no longer a girl   not yet a woman
somewhere in between

She learned to protect herself
speak his name to undo what he'd done
his scent of Old Spice
lingers in her hair   rooted in her skin

Yesterday she scarfed pills spiced with Captain Morgan
the specter boogieman
broke her into pieces
32 years later   pumped out   propped up
imperfect   damaged
her truth uncovered
she writes letters to her father
infused with Prozac, Celexa and Zoloft
whispers to mother
will she hear?
her heart a frozen muscle manages mistakes and sex

On Father's Day
Hallmark does not have the words
shame   violation   defiled   breach of trust
family secret still untold
what about sis'tah?

Did she inherit the incest gene?
Did she know what love felt like
what love looked like?
tumbling into adulthood
mothering another generation

Her child will not doubt her commitment
her child will not feel the fingers of invasion
her child emancipated

I Wanna say

Autumn left and winter arrived just in time
it flew in unexpected
stayed
on her porch
garden
her room

Nearly thirteen
she slid into shadowy closets
crunched behind the dresses
warm   not safe
early chill and dim shadows
her muscles tensed
worn wooden steps
creaked and moaned
against the heaviness of his feet

his whisper arrived
loud in her secrets
demands and invasive touches
she wanted to return to the womb
but mother was never there
instead she lived inside her hushed dreams

I gotta' say, it's not well with her at 16
she let go of her voice
heard an echo
cavern walls
collapsed
rocks and fissures

Her screams fell
muted the earth
golden-quilted
a blanket
comforts

Mother sat in denial
Daddy never apologized
winter stayed another 20 years

I wanna say, her journey was long
her feet went through fire
her heart raced to keep up
old skin flaked off
open wounds produced scars
lost her hair
grew bronze red
match the greenery

Mother was remorseful
daddy said, "I'm sorry"
the ending   her beginning
spring waited

I wanna say
because of absence
she learned to love
because of death   life

because in stillness

                                    a found voice

because of pain

                          understood forgiveness

FEET

Big feet
Wide feet
Long feet
Ten toes
Forward goes
Kicks a ball
Growing tall

Over desert
Through forest
On hot sand
Proudly we stand
Run a mile
Stilettoes got style

Old feet
Young feet
Hairy feet
In his slippers
Daddy's girl

Perfect World

Snapshot

The photo gray and grainy
sits encased with the rest
documented and logged
I am unrecognizable

We are ready for resurrection day
four   all dressed up
mummy buys two new hats for the girls
and measures two boys for infrequent suits

Daddy looks into his Kodak
another cloning against the expectant sky
black and white smiles locked in the lens
a backdrop to innocent times

New shoes too tight to run
in church for just one hour
walks on the avenue to show off our stuff
a classic time with a familiar family

Faded and worn
suspended on glossy photo paper
six souls saved on salvation day
one vibrant grin eroded by perfidy

Mercy extended her hand
grants clemency to me   then God
the snapshot hangs with the others
I see myself with a blameless smile

HAIR

Sitting between mummy's thighs

                              HAIR AT ATTENTION
waiting for comb and brush too tame

                                        Black and Thick
bristles scrape against
my crown

Mummy gathers and braids
                                        two on each side

one in the front
loosely hang
gracing my neck
long compared to my friends
mummy calls their hair

                    "niggar naps"

She is light
daddy is dark
we four blended

                                        kissed in textures
mixed and named
darkie, pinky, cream, coal
coffee, brown skin, yella

Her story repeats itself in me

Love Letter to My Son

I didn't want baby blue for my boy
too common
no advertisement necessary
He is extraordinary and needed yellows, oranges and green
it turned out, that he came out
blue/black, dark and smooth
not at all like me
he is his father's child

It was a sunny autumn day
my window faced the park
leaves at their peak
what would it be like for his hand to fold over mine?
as my palm sheltered his tiny fingers

The first time his skin was damaged, I forgot he was human
earth bound
Pictures in blue school uniforms
measured scrapes and scuffs
I tried too hard as a mother to protect the inside and out
a difficult lesson as I grew up with him

We spend days riding our bikes to the ocean
the swirling deep blues beckoned us to chase the constant
He never tired
The endless summers made for long memories
he learned to cook with his grandma
fish with his grandpa
and miss his mother who left him for the blue greens of the Army
night missions and dirt under her fingernails

Images with your slim frame and bony knees
absent of my hands to oil away the ashy shins
At 7, I left you on the blue Bahamian Island
tears never filled the void
Sometimes I look into the well of your brown eyes
I know it's OK
I know you understand the choices made
Now, your hand encircles mine
guiding me across the path
this boy who knew not of baby blue
wears the colors of the sky exceptionally well

Back Seat

On my motorcycle I have control
tucked behind my helmet
he fits perfectly in the back seat

He peered over my shoulder
I entered the highway
and heard his confession

Twist the throttle I touched 90
I felt a smile at my back
a shared need for speed

Regardless of the risk
he followed the course
down the looping road

                No fear of intrusion
                my truth journey unbridled
                free to map the direction

                Soaring on two wheels, flanked by God
                my feet planted in grace
                balancing mercy and hate

                I ride the winds of emancipation
                released from his power
                my father rediscovered

                on the arduous journey to forgiveness

Fall Skate Shoes

Bedford Stuyvesant in the 1950's was full of huge brownstone houses, where families with West Indian dialects of all types could be heard. All seasons of the year bicycles and skates ruled the sidewalks: big heavy metal skates with a key that you could tighten up the toes and wear the key around your neck. I had the baddest skates on the block and I enjoyed skating up and down on my side of the street, over to my tree boundary and back. Skating on Brooklyn sidewalks was like a test. Cracks, uneven pavements, bumps and roots were there to trip you up. The trick is to memorize your skate area, or if you were big, skate in the street. I was not big.

One day while sitting on my stoop inside the gate, taking a rest and admiring my skates and skating ability, a big boy from down the block came past my gate. He sounded friendly, but I scarcely looked up: it was forbidden to talk to strangers. I did manage to say "Hi" and to my horror, he stopped and asked to see my skates. I slowly took my skate key from around my neck, unscrewed the lock and handed him my skates. He walked away. I sat frozen behind the gate, as my skates disappeared down the street. Tears flooded my eyes.

I don't know how long I sat on my stoop, but soon grandpa came home and opened the gate and sat next to me. Somehow through my tears, he listened to my story. My crying ceased as grandpa gathered me in his arms. It felt reassuring to know that he cared about my skates, just as much as me. He began to walk around the neighborhood looking for my skates. He never found them; my wheels forever gone.

The next day as I sat on that very same stoop, inside the same gate, waiting for grandpa. I saw him come lumbering down the street with big heavy shiny new metal skates and a skate key hanging around his neck. That fall I didn't remove my skates from my shoes. If someone wanted to see or touch them, they had to take my feet too.

RAGE

My feet's was made to hold this earth
long and wide
Stood firm, clenched up my
big boy bulging inside
he done come when the first leaf fell
Autumn, good as any time to land
planted my toes deep in the soil
he slid out on a warm bed
a whimper slipped from his smooth pink lips

I lost my mind
bled out bruised blood
his skin black as midnight
I could not protect him
the whip of injustice
sheared his body
cries for freedom

No Peace

Righteousness mowed down
shot in the back
bolted rage emptied my body
swallowed in salty tears
no heaven can hold this river of pain

Forgiveness idles in the middle moments
in my hell there are gates
and I pray
knees bent
finger on the trigger

Blue Motorcycle

On the winds of expectation
twist the wrist
bottomless bass awakens
Canadian geese calling
the chorus complete

Leaping on black asphalt
through tented autumn canopies
seated behind my bug shield
grasp the bars

Blue obeys and nudges forward
grips the curves
squeezes against the ridge
switchbacks float by

Securely she takes the unknown path
slow motion is not her devotion
we have a need for speed

At the bend of the wind
vulnerable beside nature
I reach in

Without fear
riding past possibilities
scenes etched on my psyche

Backs on Which I Stand

I salute and pray for sons and fathers
knocked out, blocked out
Florsheim shoes and Air-Jordan's
a hoodie in the hood at the hoops
milk crates prop the unsupported
dried up tears
disguised

Scattered semen in mad black bowels
can't fill the pain of a thousand years
flesh of my flesh bears the mark

I wanna hear my grandmammas' song
music running down the salty walls
marching through cane fields
sun beats skin into ash
the sway of brown buttocks
pushing out babies and black pudding

Fill me up, spit you out
my language
generations of brown sugar blood
planted inside the feet of men
she embraces their unshed sorrow

Peace collides with appeals and dissent
unheard, ignored, push back

Did my anger keep you speechless?
matriarchal power between my legs
emancipates and balances paternal death

Patience and forbearance did not metastasize
stagnation became my middle name
along the jagged riverbed of grief
combined rage hums

I still pray for Black sons and fathers
in places made raw, petition for righteousness
draped defiantly in red, white and blue

Load

her spine carries

        family secrets

slow death

dragged down   knotted dreams

mother washes the clothes

    but the stain persists

reminder of   What?

the   Why?

left unspoken

she died
not knowing

No Name
For Caed

I was named
Re-named, un-named
FREEDOM
From a condition
Liberated to a condition

In my silent cell
Concrete floor
Bars steel cold
A number printed on
No name

No belt, no laces
Get up, shut up
Lights out
Doing time

Out of time
No way out
Hung up
Put up
Silence

Long Road

We grew together for nine months
an eruption   violent explosion
you slipped into this world
head full of hair
black and blue to become coffee

I counted all ten
pulling at the nipples
sore
sleep and shit   shit and sleep
pulling at the nipples
sore
no sleep   more shit

Your daddy said, "No"
then, "Yes"
then, "I don't know"
in and out

My nipples dripping
one-foot forward
I had to let go
watch you walk   run
fall
and up you go

RESIST

An army of black mammies
with recipes and prayers
marched across cane and cotton
rice and tobacco fields
plowed, plucked, protected
salt and peppered
fed tribes on scraps and bones

Two hundred years later
plated in uptown restaurants
stolen from Aunt Jemima

Bleached babies suckled on chocolate milk
armed another generation of oppressors
gorged on my ancestors' vigor
withered away through the long night of slavery

Black-a-fied, gender-fied
We escape to Fort Mose

I'm haunted by memories
an ancient coma

female spiritual warriors
standing in the hard truth of radical justice

Last letter to my father

Between the storm
a new wave   born
dislodge loose shells and stones
footprints rooted in silver sands
I stomp out melodies of freedom
play my tambourine
release my shackles
saturated with possibilities

I direct the choirs of cicadas and frogs
I write the script and produced a new movie
the forgiveness road, blocked with boulders
open sores
fiery rivers
decades to hammer
piss in the river
Thank you, daddy my greatest teacher

I grew to love below the skin
into the coral reefs of you

Letters to my father packed in the suitcase
journeyed across the rivers, sea and oceans
pressed against the rocky shore
I broke off each wound
sealed and salted
the body of shaming
cleansed in the waters
my heart beats a rhythm of absolution

I stand in determination
no longer tossed with the swells
awake to an opening
done, closed, healed
perfect pieces, persevere
I see myself in him
patterns, traits

The mirror a daily reminder
shape of the nose
chiseled chin
the curve of my ear lobes

He willed me into his image
not a choice
landscape of self-discovery
new me, will be, a better him
I no longer write letters to my father

Notes

Cou-Cou (page 5) pronounced K'-OUH. A Barbadian staple, yellow corn meal steamed with chopped okra steam/cooked until corn meal is tender & firm. Served with flying fish or other fish in a sauce.

Bakes: (page 6) Fried dough (sugar, salt, flour, lard, pinch of cinnamon/nutmeg) spoon size, deep fried in oil. Best eaten hot.

Fort Mose (page 25) pronounced (moh-say): In 1738 the Spanish governor established for runaway slaves their own fortified town, Gracia Real de Santa Teresa de Mose, about two miles north of St. Augustine, Florida. Fort Mose became the first legally sanctioned free black town in the present-day United States.

Dr. Juanita Kirton earned an MFA from Goddard College (2015) in Creative Writing & Poetry and the recipient of the Goddard College Spirit Scholarship. Juanita is published in several anthologies most recently, *Alexandria Publication Online Portfolio, Exit 13 Magazine, Goldfinch Literary Magazine, Mom Egg Review, Narrative, Persimmon Tree, Pink Panther Magazine, Nasty Women Poets, Rat's Ass Online Journal, Sinister Wisdom, Stone Canoe, Terra Preta Review, Umbrella Factory, Veterans Voices Magazine* and *WORDPEACE*. She was awarded the Baker Veterans Scholarship to attend Longleaf Writing Conference, (2018) and her poem "Fall Skates" won second prize in the Dream Quest One Writing Contest (2020).

Juanita participates in workshops/retreats with Women Who Write, Women Reading Aloud and International Women's Writing Guild. She served on editorial staff for *Clockhouse Literary Magazine,* is a teaching artist with Crossing Pint Arts (arts for survivors of human trafficking) and facilitates writing workshops for Kirkridge Retreat & Study Center.

Dr. Kirton served fourteen years in US Army, employed with PA Dept of Education. Besides writing, she enjoys touring the country on her motorcycle and lives in North East PA with her spouse.

CPSIA information can be obtained
at www.ICGtesting.com
Printed in the USA
BVHW030140120920
588170BV00002B/190